Patching The Holes

By Sarah Loucks

As I carried my bucket,

Water spilling out

I began to look around me

At the people that were about.

Looking closer at their buckets

I could see that they too had holes

But the difference between them

Is theirs were patched and mine were holes

I kept walking

water spilling everywhere

But some of them stopped me

And showed me how to repair.

They showed me how to patch the holes

With love, care and self respect.

They showed me their holes

And that they too, were not perfect.

I began to patch my holes

Slowly, one by one

I learned how to contain the water

And now the repairs have begun

It has been a couple of years since I wrote my first book. At first I was proud of what I had done, but as time grew on, I began to hate the book. But I feel like it's an important piece of my past so I will continue to make it available even though it's terribly written and is difficult to read.

I wanted to change the book and fix it, but I was told that it would ruin the book for what it already is. So I figured the next best thing to fixing it, is writing another book to offer further explanation, updates and more information. The first book, My Bucket Has Holes, was a mixture of chaos and disorder. I wasn't quite sure what I wanted to write so I just threw caution to the wind and wrote what I felt like writing and how I felt like writing it. But I poured my soul into it, even if it's a little ugly.

I know that there are grammatical rules in writing and I know that I'm breaking many of them, but honestly, I don't care. I believe writing is an art and I don't believe that any art is "wrong". Even though this book isn't professional, it isn't pretty, it isn't easy to ready, it is raw and real. I am bearing my soul for the world to read so I don't really care about grammar mistakes or errors.

For this book, I have written a collection of personal essays about events in my life. Some of them are from my distant past while others are recent events. They are in chronological order.

I am sharing my story because I want people to know what it's like to have a severe mental illness. I want people to know that it is way more than being depressed. The symptoms are aggressive and it is exhausting. My behaviors are due to my mental illness which is not an excuse but an explanation. Also, oversharing is a symptom of mine so writing this book itself is driven by my need to overshare but it is incredibly therapeutic.

My First Panic Attack

I was at work when I got the call. My mom had a heart attack at work. Thankfully, she was at and worked at the hospital, so she received immediate care. My family told me that they would call me if there was an update but everything was stable. I assured my boss I could go back to work but it started to build.

The energy began to pulsate in my body. With each heartbeat, I could feel the vibrations of my anxiety thumping. I paced the floor. I couldn't stop thinking about my mom. I realized that I needed to go home. I knew I couldn't see my mom in the hospital. I know that I should have driven straight to the hospital. But instead I drove home to crawl into my bed where I could die slowly on the inside in peace. I drove home so I could fall apart.

When I got home, there was a notice on the door. We had 48 hours to come up with our rent. I knew it was coming and I was hoping the situation would fix itself somehow but it hadn't. We were low on food, behind on all of our bills and we were surviving off of my part time job. The notice on the door hit me in the gut.

When I walked in the door, I could barely speak to my husband. I couldn't stop pacing and my heart was beating out of my chest. I wanted to curl up in fetal position and sob until my face hurt. But for some reason I couldn't cry. Nothing came out.

My husband suggested we all go to the pool. Like a zombie, I put on my bathing suit and followed my family to the pool. I was of no use to my husband as all I did was drift off into my own world, lost in my anxious thoughts. We returned to the apartment and I suggested that we all watch a movie together. Then my husband reminded me that my daughters were leaving in an hour. They were to go back to their fathers house.

All of my emotions came out at once and the energy under my skin came out as a loud moan and involuntary sobbing. Sobbing so hard that it became silent except a hiccup to breathe. My kids were in the living room. My husband helped me walk to the bedroom and he closed the door. I dropped to the floor and began to hyperventilate. I saw myself kneeling on the floor. I talked to myself.

"Calm down calm down."

But I couldn't calm down

It felt like it would never end. I believed I would never stop. I thought I was going to suffocate.

My husband didn't know what to do. This had never happened before. He asked me questions and tried to help me but he couldn't get through to me. I was completely out of control. Then, my breathing began to slow. My chest stopped thumping. My body relaxed. I melted to the floor and every inch of my body relaxed. I laid on the floor and breathed in and out. I just breathed. It had been ten minutes.

My mind slowed down. I remembered my children. I was so embarrassed. I didn't know what was going on. I got in bed and closed my eyes. I just breathed. Eventually I came out of the room although I felt weak and fragile. My husband arranged for my girls to stay another night. We did our nails and watched a movie. I visited my mom in the hospital the next day.

A Personality Problem

When I first met with a psychiatrist in 2015, I brought in a list of symptoms and a self diagnosis of bipolar. I knew that my opinion had little weight however I was the best source of what my condition was, so I wanted to get everything out on paper. When I gave him the list, he rolled his eyes and tossed it back across the desk at me. He told me that I did not have bipolar but I had a "personality problem". I was incredibly offended because to be quite honest, his bedside manner was atrocious and it was apparent that HE had a personality problem.

My therapist brought up Borderline Personality Disorder three months into therapy. She at first said that I did not have it and she described the classic borderline (confrontational, dramatic). I laughed and told her that I absolutely did not have BPD because I had bipolar. And the symptoms of BPD are terrible and they describe a really undesirable person and a bad friend. I didn't believe I was a bad friend. I thought I was at least halfway mature and BPD seemed to be a very immature diagnosis. My therapist agreed.

Nine months later she brought it up again. This time, she seriously asked me to consider the BPD diagnosis. I didn't entertain the idea for a second. There was no way I had this bogus disorder that I'd never even heard of until it was brought up. I didn't have any of the symptoms. I brushed it off and I was offended that she would even consider that diagnosis for me.

4

In 2017, I was reviewing court documents and found a summary of my medical history. It showed that I had been officially diagnosed with Borderline Personality Disorder in 2015 when I had originally met with a psychiatrist. The "personality problem" was actually a personality disorder. I was evaluated again by another psychiatrist who confirmed the diagnosis. Later on, a psychiatrist at a hospital also confirmed the diagnosis.

When I discovered this information I was pissed. I was angry that no one told me. But when I thought about it, I realized that they had tried to tell me. I was just stubborn. I wasn't ready to accept the diagnosis yet. I'm not sure I would have ever accepted the diagnosis had it not been in black in white in front of my eyes. I went straight to my current psychiatrist and he confirmed the diagnosis. And then we laughed with each other at my silly behaviors and past emotional breakdowns. It was the first time I saw myself from far away and it was tragic but hysterical at the same time.

BPD is usually comorbid with other mental illnesses as well as trauma, especially childhood trauma. In a study, it was found that the participants overwhelmingly self-perceived emotional neglect in their childhood and some psychiatrists believe that chronic emotional invalidation in childhood is a contributing factor to the development of BPD.

Those with BPD often experience severe and rapid mood swings as well as a deep fear of abandonment that causes them to act out to avoid being abandoned. BPD individuals are often extremely clingy and "suffocating" in relationships. They lack emotional permanence so when they partner or friend is not with them, they believe that the person no longer loves them. This results in a lot of "Are you mad at me?" questions and a painful feeling when left completely alone. Boredom is also a struggle as BPD individuals and their poor impulse control sometimes results in self injury, drug use or other self sabotaging and impulsive behaviors.

A pattern of intense and turbulent relationships is usually present in BPD as the individual struggles with "black and white thinking". When a person with BPD loves something, they REALLY love it. Maybe it was a party, a person, or themselves, but they can only see the good of the person/place/thing. If they are idealizing their partner, they believe that their partner is nearly god like. Their partner can do no wrong. The person with BPD could be asked to commit a crime to please their partner and most with BPD wouldn't hesitate to please them. But then they split. Something happens. Maybe there was an argument or the person simply splits for no apparent reason. If it is in a relationship, the BPD individual is half a step away from hating their family member/friend/partner. The way they breathe irritates the person with BPD. Their worst qualities are glaring. The person with BPD only sees the bad parts and often isolates themselves from the person or throws away a project that was once loved. A lot of relationships in the BPD individuals life are switched back and forth between love and hate.

Some people with BPD have a "favorite person" or "FP". This concept is strictly within the BPD community and is not recognized officially however it is such a common occurrence that it is an actual thing. This relationship is complicated. The person with BPD goes back and forth between idealizing the person and devaluing them. Often, the FP is a person that cares very little for the person with BPD however the person with BPD still makes desperate attempts to connect with the FP in any way possible. I will elaborate on this further.

A person with BPD often has an unstable self image or sense of self. They may not be quite sure what their values are and they may change from day to day. They may change goals frequently or careers. Some also question their sexuality and their own likes and dislikes. A person with BPD may not feel like they have a place in the world. They likely have horrendously low self esteem that can only be described as rock bottom.

Recurring thoughts of suicide are also present. A shocking 80% of individuals with BPD will attempt suicide at least once in their life and sadly 10% of individuals with BPD will complete suicide. Self harm is also extremely common. It is said that "all cutters have borderline and all borderlines cut". When replacing "cut" with some other form of self injury, this is very true from what I have seen. Self injury in the teen years is a hallmark for BPD.

BPD individuals also may experience a chronic feeling of emptiness. This can only be described as emotional torture that has brought me to tears. Feeling empty has haunted me to the point of a breakdown because I was bored and the empty feeling took over. This is a constant feeling. Along with rapid mood swings (which last hours or days), BPD individuals also experience intense anger and difficulties controlling their anger. This may result in broken dishes, slammed doors and an anger explosion which some even blackout during and do not remember the event after it has occured.

Dissociation is also present in many individuals with BPD. This is a feeling or experience of being outside ones body. This is a learned coping mechanism as the person is effectively turning off their emotions and state of mind to find a place of calm and comfort.

When I was first diagnosed, I read a lot. I wasn't told anything by my therapist or psychiatrist. All they did was confirm that I had BPD. I went home and started reading. I didn't know what any of the symptoms meant and I did a lot of self reflection. I learned that the nature of BPD is severe and it is seen as a complicated, if not an impossible case. Many people that I have talked to are unable to work, maintain relationships or friendships and some have even had family raise their children because their symptoms of BPD were too severe. My BPD controls my thoughts every waking moment of my day.

BPD used to be seen as an impossible disorder that some professionals refused to work with. New therapies have come out that are showing positive results for many individuals with BPD. However, these therapies are expensive, not available in all areas and may not work for everyone. And sadly, statistics show that while certain therapies may indicate an individual with BPD is recovered, many will continue to struggle as they fall back into their old habits once they graduate from the therapy. BPD is treatable, but due to finances, geographical location or other reasons, many do not have access to the proper treatment and for those that do go through the programs, they have a chance of relapsing which increases as time goes on.

Daniel

When I was reading about the concept of an FP, I began to think back on my life before my diagnosis. I went through my boyfriends and saw that I had this relationship with them. I also saw that all of my major friendships were with girls that were abusive to me and controlling, but I adored them and would do anything to please them. But, thinking back to my most glaring gcase of an FP, I realized the Daniel had been my FP.

I had been working at COV for two years when Daniel was hired. I was very attracted to him but not in a sexual way. It was an odd feeling and I couldn't describe it. I felt a need to be close to him at every opportunity so I started to arrange my schedule so I could be in the same room as him. I kept track of where he was at and what he was doing.

We began texting back and forth during work to laugh at coworkers or help each other out. One day he made a sexual joke involving me. I was hooked. It was like my heart saw an opportunity and jumped. Our text messages continued to be work related. We sometimes talked about movies or music.

Over time, I began to smother him. When I would send him a message, I would check my phone dozens of times until he responded. It could be a simple office question and I would be obsessed with getting the prized response. If it took too long for him to respond, I would lash out at others and become suicidal. During emotional breakdowns, I would send him dozens of long and lengthy text messages. Sometimes, I would begin to hate him and even delete his number.

But once he responded, my heart leapt, I fell back "in love" and my life was fabulous once again. My mood lived and breathed on his attention towards me. I had never felt this way about anyone. I thought it was love. I thought we were going to run away and get married.

In reality, I was simply his coworker. Our communication was strictly platonic at all times. Occasionally (once every six months) he would drop a flirtatious comment and it was like pouring gasoline on my bonfire of love for him. I came across his address one day at work and I wrote it down. I began to drive past his house at night to see what he was doing at home. I wanted to be able to imagine him at home and I wanted to know his life outside of work. I was sure that he wouldn't mind.

I hung on his every word. He began to pull away from me which only encouraged me to try harder. He began to arrange his schedule to avoid me, so I found excuses to find him and I teased him about it. He stopped responding to my messages so I sent more messages, and more. I was sure that he loved me, he just didn't know it yet. We were meant to be together and I just had to show him. He was just naive and I knew the truth all along. Or so I thought.

Daniel was my FP. I idealized him and I created an entire relationship which didn't actually exist. Then one day, I stopped caring about him. I no longer had a connection with him. He meant nothing to me. I had just met my husband.

My husband

After my first marriage ended, I was on a manic spree. I barely slept and I sought out men to sleep with and I filled my time with binge drinking and socializing. My self esteem was sky high and I felt like I was finally living the life I was meant to live. For five months, I was single and nearly out of control (however I still managed to make it to work most of the time). The self sabotaging was plentiful.

I joined a roller derby team. I had seen them around town and ran into them one night at the bar. They were doing shots and discussing their recent parking lot brawl. I wanted to be them. They were beautiful and strong. They were funny and seemed to have a great bond. I found out the practice time and place and I began to attend roller derby practice twice a week.

I was in the newbie group where I was learning how to roller skate but I eventually caught on and I was cruising around with moderate confidence. A few months in and a group boating trip was planned. It was a slow moving river and inflated boats. I signed up because I couldn't pass up the opportunity.

When we all got to the river the day of the trip, we were instructed to pick a boat which held up to 8 people. The group I had carpooled with grabbed a boat so I followed. A couple more people joined us. One of them was this guy that I didn't like.

When I first saw him at roller derby practice, he was surrounded by women. His name was Mike. I had heard rumors about him that painted a negative picture already. I really didn't like him even though I didn't know him. I only ever saw him from a distance.

The day of the trip, he jumped in our boat with a lit cigarette. The instructor asked him to please put the cigarette out lest it burn a hole in the boat and we all drowned. His carelessness made me dislike him even more. He put the cigarette out and we continued on. He was very drunk and blurted out funny responses. He also was very flirtatious. He was clever, friendly and encouraging. We rearranged our seating at one point and we ended up sitting next to each other. We talked and he showed me that he was actually a nice person.

As we floated down the slow moving river, the boat drifted towards the bank where a large log stuck out above the water. The boat was heading straight for it and we were all going to be clotheslined. So I sat on the edge of the boat and stuck my feet over the edge. Once we reached the log, I used my legs to push us away from the log. The boat was pushed away safely however I fell in the river.

I had a panic attack in the water and I thought I was going to kick a dead body. I was hyperventilating and I couldn't swim or focus. All I could do was panic. Thankfully I was wearing a life vest.

He immediately began to talk to me from the boat. He assured me that I was going to be okay. He helped me focus enough to swim towards the boat and I caught up to it. I grabbed onto the rope but I couldn't pull myself into the boat because of the panic attack. Before I could even try to climb up, he grabbed the straps of my life vest and pulled me into the boat. As I slid into the boat, he slapped my ass. I was infuriated.

So I quickly got up and sat next to him. I punched him in the arm as hard as I could. It hurt my hand. He looked at me with pure shock. He seemed to be completely sober at that point. We arrived at the ending of the trip soon after and we headed towards the bus. As I walked, he got my attention and came over. He apologized. He said he felt really awful about what he had done and he had gotten way too drunk. I thanked him for saving me. I forgave him.

A few weeks passed and we began to talk at practice. I learned that he was a referee. He wasn't the person that I thought he was. He was funny and nice. He listened to me and he did whatever he could to make me smile. We got to know each other over a matter of a couple of weeks and by our third date I had fallen in love.

The morning after a bar party, he was driving me back to my car. Once we arrived back at the parking lot where I had left it, I found that my window had been busted in and my skate bag had been stolen. I was devastated. I called my dad who came and took care of the window. I was driven home where I promptly crawled in bed and I didn't leave it for three days. Mike stayed by my side the whole time and he never really left. When I question my diagnosis or why he is still with me despite my issues, he reminds me of the window and how he had stayed with me during a depressive episode when we didn't even know what it was. He reminds me that I have always been this way. We have been together for seven years now and married for four.

I confessed to him once that I hated him sometimes. I found myself going through phases where I would die for him. I love him beyond normal limits. I hung on his every word. But then something would happen and I would find myself hating him. His breath would make me gag and when he touched me I would recoil. I loathed him. It was awful. So I told him how I felt. But I also told him how I had always done that in my relationships but he was the first person that I still genuinely loved while hating. I fought my thoughts of devaluing him because I wanted to be with him. I forced myself to stay. And then one day, I would return to idealizing him again.

This cycle continues to this day. I idealize him more than I devalue him. Sometimes it's caused by an event but sometimes I "split" for no reason. When this happens, I tell him. I confess that I don't like him right now and he gives me space while I try to combat my negative thoughts and my desire to push him away.

Emetophobia

I have an early memory of being about 10 and sitting in the floor of someone's living room. A young child was sitting in my lap and they threw up. I have another memory of throwing up 21 times when I had food poisoning. The times I have thrown up are burned into my brain.

The fair, drunk people, shared food and even a simple gas pain are all triggers. I fear throwing up more than I fear my own death. I cannot stand to be around someone throwing up. I have ran out of houses before because someone in the house started to throw up. So I run away.

It started when I was a child, I don't know what age. Over time, it has gotten worse.

When I wake up in the morning, my heart is pounding. I know that it's coming. The nausea starts early, usually within an hour of being awake. Sometimes it is manageable and I can function well enough to get my son to school.

Sometimes I can't function. The nausea grows more intense which causes me to become anxious which causes me to feel nauseous which causes me to feel anxious. I sometimes reach a point in the morning when I am deep breathing, laying on the floor, trying to not throw up. The thousands of intrusive thoughts of violent vomiting fill my head and it feels like my stomach wants to explode through my throat. I can't eat usually. I feel weak and dizzy often due to lack of food. If I run to the toilet, nothing happens. I've tried sticking my fingers down my throat. It lasts for 3-5 hours every day.

However, I noticed that when I'm busy, it doesn't happen as much. It's better on the weekend when my family is home. I realized that it is anxiety. I realized that my anxiety was causing me to be nauseous, not that I was anxious because I was nauseous like I thought. Now that I have better understanding of it, I know how to handle it and how to cope. I still have food aversions and panic attacks and dry heave but I feel more in control of it.

My Worst Panic Attack

I was sitting on my son's bedroom floor in my pajamas. My morning coffee was on his table and we were playing school on the floor. Then it hit me. The nausea started fast on this day. I went from completely fine to deep breathing within five minutes. It got worse. I had to stop playing and I told my husband I was going to go lay down.

I was so dizzy that I barely made it to the bed. I was afraid to lay flat so I sat up and breathed slowly. It didn't help. It was getting worse. The urge to vomit was unlike anything before. I was afraid to talk. I was afraid to breathe. I decided that it was time to go to the bathroom.

I paced the bathroom for a few seconds before I took off my glasses and pulled back my hair. I didn't want to throw up but I didn't know what else to do. I felt like I couldn't breathe without vomiting. I kneeled in front of the toilet and covered my eyes with my right arm. And I waited.

And waited.

Nothing happened.

Then I felt like I lost control. I began to cry because I was in so much pain but my cry became deep and powerful. I moaned so loud that I was yelling. My cry became so intense that it was silent. I fought the urge to smash my head into the porcelain but it was difficult. I couldn't stop crying. I rocked my body back and forth, back and forth. Eventually I laid down on the dirty bathroom floor.

I wanted to scream for my husband but I couldn't get the words out. I regretted locking the bedroom door. I wanted my husband so badly. I felt paralyzed and I felt like I was going to die.

Then my breathing slowed. I laid on the bathroom floor as my saliva and tears formed a pool around my mouth. I breathed and tried to calm down. But it started again. I began to hyperventilate as I smashed my face into the bathroom floor. My snot and tears covered my face and I sobbed so hard that my face began to cramp. I felt like I was suffocating.

Then my breathing slowed again. I laid on the floor, terrified that it would start back again. I breathed in and out and cried quietly as my heart rate slowed. I wanted to stand up but I was too weak. I laid on the floor for several minutes and then I was able to get on my knees and pull myself up. I opened the door and walked into my bedroom. Ten minutes had passed.

I headed for the living room where I found my husband. My face was soaked and I was crying so hard that I couldn't talk. I was traumatized. I was shaking and begging him to help me. He grabbed my hand and we went outside. He showed me the new tomatoes in the garden as the baby cucumbers that were growing. We sat on the swing and I just cried while he sat with me. I just wanted him to be with me.

My girls

My childhood dream had always been to be a mother. I had it all planned out; I had names, nursery themes and even the year that I wanted to have my children. But what I didn't plan for was having multiple mental illnesses. In fact, I didn't come to the realization that anything was wrong until I was 30 years old. I had three children and a happy marriage. I was elbow deep in the career of my dreams, a Behavior Therapist. But, I was completely unaware of the chaos that surrounded me. Then, it happened. I had a manic episode and in June of 2015, I lost my career and my education came to an indefinite halt.

My diagnosis was Bipolar Disorder, Borderline Personality Disorder and Generalized Anxiety Disorder. My life became a cycle of med trials and error, therapy, self care and trying to cope with my symptoms. As my semi-hibernating mental illness came to the surface, my symptoms of paranoia became worse as well as my depression, anxiety, panic attacks and my phobia to vomit (Emetophobia) grew out of control. I was in and out of the hospital, I refused to leave my bedroom and I became a shell of a person.

Meanwhile, my children stood by. When they asked where I went while I was at the hospital, they were told that I was being watched by doctors. They were told that mommy has something wrong with her brain. I described the way it feels to be sad for no reason. I told them that sometimes I get scared of little things or even nothing at all. They made me handmade cards and colored me pictures. But they saw me. They saw me fall apart and they saw me lose my will to live.

Mental illness is no stranger to my family, and it is known that my great-grandmother had to help raise her siblings because her mother had severe depression and was bed bound sometimes. Just like mental illness running in my family, anger and resentment are also present. As the mother with a mental illness became more ill in her 20's or 30's, she had children to care for.

These women of my family had little resources and while some tried treatment like electric shock therapy, they were still very ill and unable to adequately care for their children. So the oldest child raised the younger siblings, even "combing the girl's hair with a fork" at one time. The oldest child began to resent the mother and over time an ugly relationship formed of a neglected daughter and a mentally ill mother. The unhealthy relationship between the mother and children (especially the oldest child) grew well into adulthood and continued throughout their life. My grandmother still has few words to say about her mother besides her struggles with depression and anorexia.

Two years ago, my ex-husband called me. Our two daughters were afraid to ask, but they had their eyes set on a private school near his house, in his town. This school had always been a topic so this was not a new idea. We had talked about it before. I thought for a while. I weighed my options. After 9 months of going back and forth, I finally agreed to the change. I would go from having them 70% of the time to a mere 30% of the time. While they used to live at home Monday through Friday, they now visit on the weekends.

I knew that making this decision would mean sacrificing 70% of their childhood. I knew that I would miss out on Tuesday night homework and Wednesday morning ear aches. My chances of being present when they start their first period are 2 in 7. I know I will miss a lot.

But I also know that they saw a lot. They saw me slam doors off of hinges and they watched me walk into the suicide crisis center far too many times. They saw me cry for no reason and have an anxiety attack because I felt nauseous. They've watched me struggle to climb out of a hole and they watched me fall back in several times.

I knew that I had put in the effort to be an active parent in their life. I tried Girl Scouts once. I volunteered to be a troop leader which turned me into a manic catastrophe and it ended with me ignoring phone calls and emails and the whole group falling apart while I was depressed in bed. I wanted my children to experience the childhood that my parents had given me. I wanted them to have extracurricular activities, friends, safety, security and most of all, a stable parent. As much as I tried, I could not give them stable. Instead, I gave them a mother that spent weeks in bed and has sobbing fits like a hormonal teenager. I showed them how to not react when you are angry. I showed them how to fall apart.

So when this decision was presented to me, I immediately considered what was in their best interest. Of course they wanted to attend the school but they were good students and I knew they would excel in any environment. Having them on the weekends would mean more leisure time and family trips. We would also have them for every holiday too. But my only concern was them and my mental health. As they grow older and become more aware, the little things will leave an impression on them. I knew they would watch me struggle and scramble trying to care for myself and them as well. I knew I would fall on my face and they would suffer. I would become my great-grandmother and my great-great-grandmother. I knew that I would be laying in bed and one day my daughter would have to use a fork to comb her sister's hair and I knew that the family tradition would continue.

It has been almost a year since we changed schedules. Some days I'm okay with it. I'm thankful for the time to go to therapy, support groups and to focus on my well-being. I'm thankful for the opportunity to take care of myself, so I can be a better mother for them. But there are also the nights that I crawl into their little bed and I sob until my eyes burn. I question my decision constantly and I am stuck in the endless cycle of not wanting to harm them but also wanting to maintain a healthy relationship with them despite being mentally ill. At times, my anxiety keeps me home, but I try to attend every competition, ceremony, play and recital. We send pictures to each other and I am creating a scrapbook of memories for them to keep at their house.

I don't know if I will ever be settled with my decision and I feel like I will always be in turmoil over my daughters and this decision. I pray that they forgive me when they are grown and I hope that my phone calls and cake baking moments are enough because that's all that I can give them.

I did it for them.

The Post-it Notes

I was standing at the kitchen sink when I felt the plug being pulled. My emotions turned to black, every ounce of energy escaped and where my soul had been was a vacant void. Everything had drained out of me and emptiness was what was left. Within minutes, I was depressed. Nothing had happened. I was simply washing dishes when the flip was switched. Sometimes there is a reason. Sometimes someone says something, or I read something and I get sent into a tailspin. Other times however, nothing happens. I am emotionally devastated for absolutely no reason. My chest physically aches. I feel overwhelmingly guilty, ashamed and devastated.

The pain is so intense that sometimes I cry so hard I lose my voice. I was in the middle of cleaning the house, my 4-year-old was expecting lunch and I couldn't go on anymore. Like a balloon with punctures, I stood there deflating until all that was left was the shell of a person who once was alive inside. It was getting bad. It was going to get worse, I could tell. My feelings started to ache. It felt like I had been made fun of in front of the whole school. I started to sob as I walked to the couch where I wrapped a blanket around me and called my husband.

"Is it bad?" he asked.

"Yeah," I said into the blanket as tears poured.

"You need me to come home?" he asked.

"But I don't want you to miss work." I said.

"That's what sick time is for. I can come home, do you need me to?" he asked.

"Yeah," I said as I sobbed into the blanket.

I hated calling him at work, but I could feel myself falling and I had a child who needed me. I knew I had a matter of hours before everything got dark. He came home to me sitting in the same spot where I called him earlier. I didn't greet him. I didn't touch him. I simply walked down the hall to our bed, undressed and crawled into the blankets. I curled up in fetal position and stared at the wall. For hours, I stared at the same spot. My mind was loud. I told myself what a loser I was. I told myself I was an idiot for not working. I was ashamed of my life. I was mortified. I mentally attacked myself. Because I knew all of my own insecurities, I knew exactly what to say and what to bring up, so I won. I attacked my weaknesses and I attacked where I was the most self-conscious. I brought up ancient heartaches and relived each one. I tortured myself with shame, sadness and pain. I hated myself.

I could hear my family living outside of the bedroom. I could hear the children laughing, I could hear my husband singing to the radio, I could smell dinner cooking. They talked and laughed. My heart ached. I wanted so badly to get up and join them. I wanted to know what they were laughing about. I wanted to see what was for dinner. I wanted to breathe in the scent of the food and taste the sun tea that was sitting outside. I wanted to laugh with them. But I couldn't. My knees were folded against my chest and my arms were brought in to my chest where

I clenched my fists around the blankets and laid there on the bed, completely still. My husband checked on me every few hours and I remained still. Only my eyes moved as I blinked.

I laid there for hours. I laid there for days. I didn't change my clothes. I didn't brush my hair. I didn't brush my teeth. I laid there and listened to my own voice tell me what a useless loser I was and what a weak excuse for a human being I was. I screamed at myself to just get up. I shouted at myself to stop being such a loser and get out of bed. But I couldn't. I just laid there. One day at around 6 a.m., when the sun is still weak but grows brighter as each minute passes, I put my feet on the floor and stood up. My short curly hair was chaos, my breath smelled like rotting meat. My clothes smelled like body odor. I wrapped my favorite blanket around my shoulders and stood up, taking a few steps forward. Everyone in the house was sleeping. All the children were spread out on their beds, snoring away. My husband laid behind me in the bed where I had laid. I decided to head down the hall for water, so I came out of the room and began to walk down the hall, but then I saw it. So I stopped. There was yellow everywhere. Small yellow sticky notes were stuck to the wall. They were everywhere. The entire hallway was lined from top to bottom with small notes. I began to read them.

"You are not a burden."

"You matter."

"You are wanted."

"You are enough."

"I'm so glad you're here."

"You make my life better just by being in it."

"No matter how dark your days are, I'm here for you."

"I love you."

"I'll give you time and I'll be here when you're ready."

I began to sob as I found such comfort in his notes. "What?" he said from behind me. I sobbed and walked to him where he wrapped his arms around me. "You did this for me?" I asked, still crying. "Yes," he said. This was not unusual for him to do. He had always left me love notes, written poems on the mirrors and bought me little trinkets. But this time I desperately needed to read the notes. For days my mind had been screaming at me and I was so weak. I felt like I could only crawl out of the hole. My soul was so raw and beaten, bruised and sore. I had no life left in me. I had no desire to be alive. I had no will power to exist. My heart ached, my eyes burned from crying. I was in a dark tunnel, alone. I didn't know which direction I was going in or where I was going because it was so dark. But suddenly at the end of the tunnel appeared a hallway of yellow sticky notes. My husband hugged me tight and I wiped away my tears. He told me he had wanted to help me, but he didn't know how. So he came up with this idea a while ago, he was just waiting for the right time to do it and he did it last night. I left the notes on the wall until the glue started to dry and they began to fall on the floor. I kept about 20 of my favorites and taped them to the wall next to my bed. It's the first thing I see in the morning and the last thing I see at night. Every day his notes remind me that I'm not a burden, my existence is not causing my family pain, I am not a loser and I am loved. I am so loved.

Breakdown

I woke up one morning to a text message. My husband needed me to go to the bank as soon as I could. Once I started to wake up and move around, I could feel that something was off. I felt like a bad mood was just over the horizon. I felt the need to prepare for the storm so I quickly picked up the house and headed straight to the bank so I could take care of the problem.

I could feel myself melting to the floor as I stood in line. It took all of my strength to not lay down on the floor. It was excruciating to stand in line and by the time I was at the front, I was near tears. Unfortunately, the teller explained that there was a problem however nothing could be done. I began to cry out of frustration and I left the bank. I got to the car and called my husband crying.

I sobbed into the phone and explained the situation. He had to ask me several times to repeat myself because I was crying so hard. I was afraid to drive home because I couldn't stop crying and I had no motivation to even walk, let alone drive a car. He gave me confidence and helped me calm down. After a while, I decided that I was well enough to drive back across town so I headed home.

My eyes were full of tears. I drove silently hoping just telling myself that I was almost there. I was so weak and I just wanted to lay down and cry. I got halfway home and I was sitting at a stop light in a busy intersection.

As the light turned green, I gave the car gas but it didn't budge. I tried again and again. I looked at the gauges and saw that it was too hot. I put the flashers on and began to sob as I sat in the middle of the street blocking traffic in the left lane.

A few minutes later, I heard a light tap on my window and a guy offered to help me move the car. I wiped away my tears and he pushed my car off the road. I called my dad for emotional support. I knew what needed to be done, I had driven a car like this before, but I just needed someone to be there with me. He got to my car and helped me fix it enough to get it home.

I finally walked in the door two hours after leaving and I collapsed in bed. My emotions were strained and I was so weak. I didn't know how long this episode would last but I decided to try to sleep it off (which sometimes works). It didn't in this case. I woke up from my nap and I laid there for an hour before I tried to get up. But I couldn't. I begged myself to get out of bed but I just laid there, staring off into space.

The depression continued for several days. I tried to wake up in the morning and be productive, but after getting my son off to school and taking care of the animals, I felt too weak to stand up. All I craved was my bed. All I wanted was to lay down. I knew that laying down would immediately soothe me and I wanted nothing else. Then one morning, the depression was gone and I began to pick up the pieces that were scattered about.

As my depression deepens, my desire to lay down increases. It becomes to intense that I have had to stop myself from laying down in the middle of a store. If I stay up, and I force myself to sit on the couch in the upright position, my anxiety becomes out of control. I usually start sobbing and I try to lay down on the couch. The weight of the blankets in my bed is soothing. The silence is soothing. When I am out of bed while depressed, I am on the verge of collapse at the slightest loud noise or comment. I am a ticking time bomb waiting to explode. In bed, my heart slows and I can breathe.

My depressions are caused by a few different factors. The first thing that causes my depressions is Bipolar Disorder. These depressions come out of nowhere, for no reason. Sometimes they are preceded with an episode of hypomania however that is very rare for me. These depressions last for weeks or months. The house falls apart as I slowly move though life in pajama pants and sips of water. After three years of medication, these depressions are now infrequent. They used to happen more than ten times a year. Now, they happen about twice a year.

My other depressions are caused by BPD. These episodes are typically started by an event or conversation. Someone says something upsetting, a simple comment or maybe a hint of disapproval. I spiral quickly and it usually lasts for hours or days. Sometimes my mood drops for no reason at all. And sometimes it will correct itself within a couple hours and my life will carry on like usual.

Having two different depressions means that it is confusing once it starts. Because both Bipolar and BPD cause me to have depressions that start out of nowhere but are also caused by events too. So when I become depressed, I never know if it's going to last for an hour or three months. Which is why when I feel a depression coming on (sometimes I know it's happening before it starts) I take care of my affairs, tie up loose ends and prepare the house for my absence while I hide in my cave. Other times however, my depressions are unprovoked and there is no warning. Just the feeling of wanting to melt to the floor, curl up in fetal position and sob until my throat becomes raw.

Empty Emotions

Imagine that our emotions are deflated balloons. Excitement, grief, anger, sadness are all there. When the balloons are empty, we do not feel the emotion. There is no need for our mind to experience these emotions when there is no cause.

When something happens (death, argument, love, etc.), these events are put inside of the corresponding balloon which causes the balloon to inflate and we feel the emotion. So if we are angry about an argument, the argument would go into the anger balloon and we would feel anger. However, sometimes I experience what I call "empty emotions". I have the same balloons as everyone else (although mine, due to BPD, are more dramatic, extreme and "bigger") but sometimes they malfunction. At times, even when nothing has happened, one or some of my balloons will inflate. I will feel the deep burning anger that one would experience if there had been a terrible fight, but no such fight had occured. My guilt balloon often inflates and I begin to feel guilty for anything and everything. Sometimes the guilt builds up so much that I have to hide in my bed because I feel guilty for existing.

When I'm experiencing empty emotions, my mind sometimes tries to find something to put inside the balloon. So my mind will desperately search for a situation in my past which could be resurfaced and placed in my balloon. This is when my brain is flooded with every time I had ever embarrassed myself or every time I have ever been angry. This causes me to be overwhelmed with my emotions and they become unbearable. Empty emotions cause me to lash out at innocent people and cry when there is nothing to cry over. I have to work very hard to control my explosive emotions which are often misplaced and empty.

Doubting my diagnosis

While I was growing up, I was a very emotional child. Living with a suicidal thoughts at the age of 13 is quite traumatizing in itself. What made it worse however were the comments around me.

"You're just being dramatic."

"You're doing it for attention."

Many people with mental illness have been told these phrases and my reaction was to internalize my shame and self doubt. Over time, I agreed with them; I was doing it for attention. So I have tried to stop a thousand times, but it wouldn't stop. One of my worst fears is that I am actually making all of this up for attention. I am just being dramatic. Deep down, this is what I truly believe.

Sometimes I become obsessed with being better. I begin to yell at myself to be a grown up and get over myself. I tell myself to stop taking my medication and stop going to therapy. I tell myself that I am being a baby and it's all for attention.

But when I stop my medication, a severe depression starts within three days or I become manic within 24 hours. I still doubt that I'm actually mentally ill but the repercussion of not taking my medication is usually enough for me to take them every day, twice a day. Not always though as I still stop my meds sometimes.

Attention

When a baby is born, they learn to communicate with their cry. When they have a soiled diaper or need a cuddle, they learn that by crying, they get their needs met. Their cry brings them help and comfort. They use their voice to have their needs met. How else are they supposed to get help?

When I am suicidal, I seek attention. I tell my husband. I may post it to facebook. I seek the attention of those around me because I seek their help. I need for them to be there for me in the time that I need them the most. When I am suicidal, I feel like I am a burden to my family. I believe that my very existence is causing them emotional pain. I believe that the only way to prevent myself from harming them anymore is to kill myself. It is the only option.

When I reach out, I need my friends and family to tell me that I'm not a burden. I need them to tell me that they love me and I need to know that I have support. I need attention and comfort. I need a friend stopping by for coffee. I need my husband to tell me that he still loves me. When I am suicidal, I need people to give me reasons to stay. I need to know that it's worth it. I need to know that I should fight to stay alive. Being given attention calms my suicidal thoughts and can sometimes even stop them altogether. Sometimes all I need is a friend to offer a different perspective or someone to vent to and I feel better. Other times, all they can do is comfort me as I try to hold on.

When people are suicidal, it is rumored that they do it for attention. They do it for pity. They do it to show off. Because it is the act of killing yourself, people blame the person for attempting suicide even though the person had fought the illness until they couldn't fight anymore. People are not suicidal for fame. They are not suicidal for pity. They are not suicidal to seem cool. When people are suicidal, they are standing on the edge of a metaphorical cliff and behind them is a fire that is creeping closer. When a person is suicidal, they are in an incredible amount of pain and agony. Their thought process is jumbled and their mind isn't clear. When people are suicidal, they may believe that it will literally never get better. They may be delusional and believe that their family is suffering simply because they exist. People are suicidal because they are mentally ill.

A person being suicidal should always be taken seriously. The very act of threatening suicide is unnatural. We are supposed to recoil when we think of our own death, not embrace it. Threatening suicide without the actual intent of committing suicide is a symptom of BPD.

I sometimes feel suicidal when I am in an extreme amount of stress. When this happens, I lose control and become fully capable of committing suicide however ultimately, I just want attention/help from my family. I don't want to die. Other times, I am actually suicidal and am in danger of hurting myself. It is difficult for me to tell the difference and impossible for an outsider to tell the difference so suicidal threats should always be taken seriously. BPD patients account for a large portion of hospitalizations and repeated suicide attempts and threats are a red flag for BPD.

My suicidal thoughts and expressions are not for pity. I do not want anyone to feel bad for me. I do not want to be seen as weak. I do not want anyone to say "Poor poor Sarah." What I want is for people to tell me that they love me and care for me. I need them to remind me that this phase is only temporary, it will be good again soon. I need people to love me louder and harder. I do not want their charity or pity. What I want is encouragement and a hug. I want to be reminded why I'm still fighting. I need someone to remind me of my middle daughter's likely reaction to finding out I have died. Her face is what I see when I am in the deep dark pit.

What I need is attention/help and love.

Writing

When I lost my job in 2015 after my major manic episode, I immediately felt guilty. I had held a job since I was 17. I have worked two jobs at once before and at the time I was working full time while also attending college full time. It was an exhausting schedule but I felt like a productive member of society. I felt like I was contributing to the world.

Losing my job resulted in me feeling an immense amount of guilt. I was no longer bring in money and I no longer left the house every day. I felt like a leech to society and those in my life. My stability bounced like a basketball so finding a job would be pointless as I would likely not even make it through the first day if I even made it to the job in the first place. But after two years of medication and therapy, things began to settle a little (or so I thought) so I began to look into what I could do. I knew that a traditional job wouldn't work for me but I needed a home based job that

I could do on my own time. Being a writer, I immediately thought of freelancing.

After some research, I found a website that hosts clients and freelancers to come together for projects. The platform allowed for communication, file exchanges and for payment to be sent as well as received. Technically, I became a self employed freelance writer and I used this platform to gather clients and projects. It was incredible.

I jumped right into it. Of course my anxiety skyrocketed due to the pressure and stress. I stopped sleeping well and I became obsessed with writing. I began to skip sleep altogether and I eventually spent 50+ hours a week typing articles for clients. The pay was little, but the productivity was major and I was on a little manic spree. I took on more clients and more clients. I juggled everything as best as I could although the house began to be neglected and I found myself skipping family activities to write, even on the weekends. It became too much.

I broke down. One day, I was typing an article and it felt like a drain had been pulled. Slowly, all my motivation and enjoyment flowed out. I was left with the feeling of exhaustion. I no longer cared about writing. At all. I quickly wrote a short email to each of my clients explaining that a "family emergency" had occured and I was going to be a little behind this week. I did not indicate how long because I was so unsure. It could be three hours, or three years.

Of course, I went to bed where I laid wrapped up like a burrito. Over the next several days I began to get emails from clients wondering where I was at. I didn't have the emotional energy to respond or have a conversation so I ignored the emails. Projects were cancelled. Clients dropped me. It was all gone.

When I was doing better, I signed back into the website to see the mess I had left. I found that my approval rating was now too low to accept jobs. I had been effectively fired. The months of writing meant nothing when I had one mental health crisis. Of course, I understand the nature of the working world and while it's not quite fair, it is realistic to think that clients would move on to other freelancers if one seems flakey or unable to complete an assignment. I understand that work must be done, with or without me.

I cried for days when I found out that I had lost my freelancing career. I had loved it so much. It had given me projects to complete, clients, conference calls, money and pride. And now it was all gone. It was all washed down the rain.

The Hospital
It started one day. I was sitting at the computer and I had the urge to Select All + Delete. I recognized the urge. I had felt it so often in my life. The second a depression hits, I want to discard whatever is in front of me. My job, my projects, my friends. I want to throw it all away and isolate myself from everything and everyone. I have learned to not delete my projects but rather to save them, and just walk away. So I did.
I headed towards the bedroom. I stared at my bed. I wanted so badly to lay in my warm blankets and cuddle up with my pillow. My only reprieve from the pain that was beginning to settle in my chest. My phone rang. I opened the video call and my husband's face appeared in his orange work vest.
"Hello my sexy beautiful gorgeous wife!" he said.
"Hello, how is work?" I asked.
He explained that there was a situation in the field and he was going to be tied up all day.
"I'm not going to be able to call so I wanted to make sure that you were doing okay." He said.
I sighed. I hated telling him. I knew that it made him worry and I wanted him to focus on work.
"I'm having a bad day." I said. "It started a little bit ago. I was writing and I just started to feel like crying for no reason. I want to just lay in bed." I said as I began to cry.
"So do it baby." he responded. "Do what you need to do. That's why you are home; so you can take care of yourself."
"I feel so guilty and lazy though. I should be productive. The house should be spotless and there is laundry to do." I began to sob and I sat on the bed. "But maybe a nap will make me feel better. It sometimes does."
"You won't be mad?" I said as I wiped away my tears and went to close the curtains. I shut the door to the bedroom.
"No. If that's what you need to do to feel better, then do it." he said.
"Okay, I'll take a nap and see if I feel better." I said.

We said our goodbyes and hung up the phone. I took off my shoes and sweater and I climbed into bed. I wrapped the blankets around my body like a burrito and I rolled to my side. My phone lit up with a message, but I didn't even care. I could hear the kids playing on the playground at the school next door and I wondered if any of them were going to be like me. I wondered which kids on the playground would be laying in bed on a weekday afternoon wishing they were dead. I hoped none of them would be like me. I felt like I was sleeping my life away. I eventually fell asleep. I woke up with ten minutes before the school bell rang. My husband had kissed me on the forehead.

"I'll be back." he said as he headed to the school to pick up our son.

I told myself to get up. I wanted to get up and be back to normal by the time they came back. I laid in bed on my back, staring at the ceiling. I begged myself to get up, but I just laid there. I could feel my bladder beginning to stretch and I remembered all the coffee I had drank all morning. I told my brain to get up, but I just laid there instead. Twenty minutes passed and I heard the front door open.

My son's voice carried down the hall. He told my husband that he had planted a sunflower at school and he had a field trip slip to be signed for the kindergarten trip to the zoo. I just laid there, eavesdropping on them. My bladder started to pulsate. I knew I had to get up. I tried again. Again and again. I daydreamed about getting up. I begged myself to at least go to the bathroom, but I couldn't. I laid there, a burrito that had to pee.

I could hear my husband and son go into the backyard. I wish my husband would come in so he could help me get out of bed.

Get up. Get up.

I felt like I was frozen.

I started to feel like I was going to lose control of my bladder. My husband entered the room and he saw me crying hysterically.

"What is it, what's wrong?" he asked.

"Why mommy crying?" my son asked.

"I need to go to the bathroom." I said and shut my eyes. I was so ashamed. I was 32 years old and couldn't get out of bed to pee.

"Uhm." he stared at me. "What do I do?"

"Please help me sit up." said in between sobs. He walked over and lifted my torso up as I spun and sat on the edge of the bed.

"I just need to get to the bathroom." I said as I planted my feet on the floor and stood up. I headed for the bathroom in hysterical tears.

"Maybe you should try sitting on the couch." he said when I came out of the bathroom.

"I can't." I said as I sat back on the bed. "I need to lay down. I'm so weak."

"Okay. I'll come in and check on you in a little while." he said as he covered me up as I laid back down on the bed.

I should have probably showered. I hadn't done so in three days so far. My leg hair was starting to catch and pull on my pants and my face was greasy. Instead, I wrapped back up like a burrito and laid in the bed. I stared off into space. I listened in on what they were doing. I could tell that they were watching tv and my son was playing with toys in the floor. I drifted off back to sleep.

I woke up to my husband shaking my foot.

"Hey" he said and smiled. "I'm going to start dinner. Pork chops. You hungry?"

I shook my head.

"Okay, well let me know if you're hungry and I'll make you a plate." he said. He walked over and kissed my forehead. "Maybe you should come out and join us. We are watching Jurassic Park."

"Maybe." I said. I already knew that I wouldn't. I was already slipping into a hole and I hadn't told him yet.

I hadn't told him that I was starting to accidentally day dream about my own death. I hadn't told him what a burden I felt like and how awful I felt about existing. I was so ashamed of myself. I thought back to a phone call with my mom and regretted what I had said. I thought back to the laundry that was piled up and I felt ashamed. I felt embarrassed of the mess I had become and so ashamed of what I had done. I cried as I heard my husband turn on the radio and start to cook dinner. I laid there for a few hours, envisioning swallowing a bottle of pills. Tying a rope to the rafters in the garage. Slitting my wrists over the shower drain so I wouldn't make a mess.

"Here" my husband said as he brought me a glass of iced tea. "Want me to make you something? You have to eat."

"Maybe." I said. I felt a little hungry. He disappeared down the hall and returned a while later with a sandwich. I untangled my arms from the blanket and took a bite as I laid in bed. It was the only bite I took.

The evening progressed and so did I. I remembered the bottle of pills in the cabinet, the ones I had hidden. I remembered the razor blade I had stashed in the bathroom. I laid there and imaginatively killed myself over and over. In between my imaginary deaths, I thought of more reasons to go through with my plan. There were so many reasons to go through with it. I could barely think of reasons to not go through with it. I was deep in thought when my husband came in the room.

"How are you doing?" he asked as he sat on the edge of the bed.

"I feel bad. I can't stop thinking of killing myself." I said as my eyes filled with tears again.

He didn't respond.

"I'm sorry. I'm not doing it on purpose. I just feel awful and I can't stop thinking about it." I said.

"Do you have a plan? Do we need to go to the hospital?" he asked.

"No, it's okay." I lied and assured him.

He invited me to come into the living room but I was too busy imagining mutilating my own body. Had I had the energy, I would have been in the bathroom with the razor blade. But instead I laid in bed and stared off into space.

Later on in the evening, after our son had gone to bed, my husband came in.

"Do I need to worry?" he asked as he headed towards his dresser.

"Maybe." I said quietly.

"What's that supposed to mean?" he asked with frustration.

"I don't know." I said. "I don't know."

"Well, should I call your mom or not?" he asked and approached me.

I began to cry as I thought of my plan. I had already set the alarm on my phone for 2:00 am. Plenty of time to swallow the pills and die on the bathroom floor. I wanted to go through with my plan. But more than that,

I didn't want to inconvenience my family. I was sure that my parents were probably already in bed. They may even be sleeping. I didn't want to wake them up.

"I'm sorry." I said as I sobbed.

"Sorry for what? What's going on?!" he demanded.

"I need to go." I said as I continued to sob. My tears mixed with my runny nose and my pillow became damp.

"Are you sure?" he asked. I hesitated for a minute. I was about to cause a commotion. I was about to embarrass myself and my family.

"Yes." I said. "I need to go."

"Okay, pack a bag. I'll walk over and talk to your mom." he said. I could tell he was angry. I knew that logically he was angry at the situation but at the time, I felt like he was angry with me. I started to cry as I unwrapped from my burrito and threw a handful of pajama clothes and underwear on the bed. I threw a book in the pile too. I put my meds in the pile. I put on my digital watch. I sat on the bed and cried.

"Here's a bag" he said as he handed me a shopping bag. "Your mom is going to stay here with Oliver while I drive you to the hospital. When I go to work tomorrow, your dad is going to come over and stay with him. It's Friday and I'm off on Monday, so don't worry."

"I'm so sorry." I sobbed. He put my clothes and book in the bag. "I'm so sorry."

"Baby, it's okay." he said as he grabbed my hand and helped me stand up. I slid my shoes on and followed him down the hall. My mom entered the front door and I didn't make eye contact. I was so ashamed. How could I be doing this again?

As we drove to the hospital, my stomach began to grumble. I remembered that I hadn't eaten a proper meal in two days. I had become a bit manic with my writing and spent my meal time writing instead of eating. I realized I was starving. I cringed. I knew what the food was like. It was literally leftover jail food. It was like they had a budget of $10 to feed the entire hospital. I began to crave fast food like never before.

"I'm hungry." I said as we drove down the street.

"I'm sorry. I tried to get you to eat. I don't have any money on me." he said. I felt awful for asking. He had already done so much for me.

30

We arrived at the hospital and I asked for a cigarette. I knew that I wouldn't be allowed to smoke until I was released and it was too late for a nicotine patch, so I would be nicotine free until the morning. I took my time finishing my cigarette before we headed inside.

I knocked on the door and a woman that I recognized opened the door. "Can I help you?" she asked.

"I need to talk to someone." I said as I cried. My husband handed me my shopping bag of clothes.

"Okay, come on in" she sighed and opened the door.

"I'm going to go." my husband said through the door opening. I nodded and he said that he loved me. The lady closed and locked the door. The sound of the door locking made my skin crawl.

"What's your name sweetie?" she asked as she began to dig for paperwork in a filing cabinet. "Have you been here before?"

I quietly explained that I had been here before, many times. They already had a file for me. She reviewed my diagnoses, my medication and asked me questions.

"Do you have a plan?" she asked as she looked over the brim of her glasses.

"Yes." I said and closed my eyes.

"Can you tell me about that plan?" she asked.

"There's pills in the cabinet at home. And the knives are sharp. I wanted to slit my wrists but also stab myself. I really want to stab myself." I confessed. "But I was going to wake up at 2 am and swallow the bottle of pills."

"In the bathroom." I added.

"Okay." she said as she jotted down some notes. "Go ahead and go into the patient room. I'm going to go talk to the doctor." I walked into the patient room as she headed out the door.

I knew the routine. She was going to talk to the doctor and the doctor was going to put me on a hold. I had to spend 24 hours in the patient room at the crisis center before they would officially admit me to the hospital. I never understood the reasoning behind the 24 hour waiting period but I knew the rules.

The lady came back and gave me some papers to sign.

"Okay hon, we have you on a hold. You'll be in here until this time tomorrow and then we will send you to the back. So make yourself comfortable." she said. She handed me some paperwork to sign that involved my rights as a patient and signing in my inventory of belongings I had brought. She handed me the tv remote and left the room. I put the remote on the floor and instead pulled back the blankets on the bed and laid on the cot. I loved the blankets. They were thick and heavy. My stomach growled.

I opened up my phone and scrolled through social media. I was starving and I had stupidly announced that I was going to be going to the hospital so now my friends and family were sending messages of love and support while I stared at my phone in embarrassment. I deleted the post. My stomach growled.

I typed a post.

"If anyone could bring me a burrito, that would be fantastic."

A local friend responded.

"Where are you?"

I told her the hospital name. I didn't think she was serious.

"Okay, I'll be there in twenty minutes." I was shocked. And I was so excited. I spent twenty minutes waiting for my burrito which distracted me from the pain.

She arrived in the door with the fast food and she was directed to my room. She smiled ear to ear when she saw me. I was so happy to see her.

She sat with me for an hour. She confessed that she too had spent time in this hospital at one point in her life. She explained how she was feeling back then and what she had gone through. I got teary eyed as she explained her emotions and reasoning. I didn't talk very much. I just listened and ate my burrito. She brought me a soda too.

Soon I was finished eating and she was ready to go. She said goodbye and I stood up to hug her. My stomach was full and I was so thankful to see her. I didn't want her to leave. I wanted her to stay. But she left. It was late.

The room was quiet and empty again. I laid in the bed. The reality set in. I had 22 hours to lay in this cold and quiet room. I wanted to leave. I had to get out. But I knew I had to stay. I pulled the blankets over my face and I cried until my eyes were swollen. I nodded off a few times but the majority of the night was spent crying or staring off into space and fixating on death.

The shift change happened at 7am so I waited for it to quiet down before I went out of the room.

"Do you need something?" the man compassionately asked behind the desk.

"I want to go home." I said. I had been thinking about it for hours.

"What do you mean? Have a seat." the man pointed to the chair next to the water fountain. I sat down.

"I feel better. I want to go home." I said. I lied. I had done this in the past. When they ask if I'm doing better, I say yes because all I want is to go home. So I tell them what they want to hear. He asked me a few more questions and then headed to the back where he would talk to the doctor. I sat back in the room. I sent my husband a text message.

"I might be coming home."

"Why?"

"I want to come home. It's our anniversary."

"Okay, let me know."

The man entered the room a few minutes later and asked to talk to me. I followed him and sat back down in the chair.

"So do you feel like you're going to hurt yourself anymore?" he asked.

"No" I lied.

"Do you have access to any of the things you had access to before you came? Can your family make the house safe for you?" he asked.

"No and Yes." I said.

"Okay, I'm going to go back talk to the doctor and I'll be right back. He left the room and I sat on the bed. I was shaking. I wanted to go home so bad. I didn't even remember why I had come in the first place. All I wanted was to go home. The man returned with a paper in his hand.

"Okay, do you have family you can contact to pick you up? You can use our phone. I will need to talk to them too. I'll need you to sign this before you go." he said. I knew what it was. It was a contract that I wouldn't hurt myself and if I felt like I needed to, I would come back. I signed the paper, made the call and waited in the chair for my husband to show up. It took about twenty minutes before I heard a car pull up in the parking lot followed by a knock on the door. The other employee opened the door and reminded me to come back if I needed to. I said goodbye and they locked the door behind me.

The sun was bright. I felt like a vampire. The heat was hot. The noise of the city was loud. I wanted to get back in bed. My husband walked me to the car and I got in. I lit up a cigarette and we headed towards home. I couldn't wait to go home and get back in bed. Before I knew it, we were in the parking lot of the mini mart.

"What are we doing?" I asked with anger.

"I'm just getting a soda. Come with me. I'll get you a coffee." he said.

"I don't want to." I responded.

"Come on." he encouraged me. I decided to go with him.

But as soon as we entered the door, I wanted to run back to the car. I wanted to go home. I wanted to be in my burrito. We headed back to the car after getting our drinks and I put mine in the cup holder. I didn't even want it.

Once we got home, I told him I wanted to go to bed. He begged me to try to stay up. I agreed and we went to the backyard to sit under the mulberry tree. I sat my coffee on the patio table.

"I'm going to go get Oliver from your dad." he said. He left me in the backyard where I sat half alert. I wanted to go back. I felt fragile. I felt like I was going to completely lose control any second. Every alarm in my head was going off and I knew that I needed to go back. All my thoughts got worse and I knew I had to tell him.

"I think I need to go back." I said once my husband and son returned.

"What? Why?" he asked.

"They told me to come back if I need to and I think I need to. I'm going to lose it. I feel like I'm going to break." I responded.

My son played with a toy near us as we talked and my husband tried to convince me to stay. He didn't understand why I wanted to go back. But he didn't understand that it wasn't that I wanted to go back but rather,6 it was that I had to. As my son twirled around with his toy, he bumped into the table and my coffee spilled everywhere. I immediately began to sob profusely and I couldn't calm down no matter how many times I said it to myself.

"Baby don't cry, I'll get you more coffee." He said desperately.

"I need to go back." I said in between tears.

"Fine." he growled in frustration. "Get your stuff. I have to take Oliver with us this time."

I went inside and grabbed my bag that I had sat on the table, still packed. We headed to the car and took the main street towards the hospital. I cried all the way there. I didn't want to go back.

"Okay, I can't go in with you this time." he said as he glanced in the rearview at our son.

"I know." I said as I wiped away my tears. "I love you." I said and gathered my things.

"Where's momma going?" My son asked.

"I'm going to go see a doctor." I said and forced a smile.

I kissed my son and knocked on the door of the crisis center. Just like last time, the woman opened the door and I entered the room as she locked the door behind me.

I sat in the chair and cried.

"What happened?" the guy at the desk said.

"I had to come back. I lied. I don't feel better. I just wanted to go home." I said.

"Ah, I see. Well, go ahead and make yourself comfortable. We'll have to do the intake process over again. You'll have to repeat the 24 hours." he said.

"Really?" I asked. "I was gone for like an hour."

"Yep, you have to start over." he said as he handed me the forms to sign. I signed the paper and headed to the room. I sat back down on the bed that I had sat on only an hour before. I laid down and pulled the blanket over me. I quickly fell asleep. I was exhausted.

I woke up to the door opening and someone bringing in a plate of food.

"Lunch" they said as they sat the plate down on the table. It was iceberg lettuce, a piece of bread, a bowl of soup and a carton of milk. I grumbled and rolled over. I spent the next 24 hours fading in and out of sleep. I would either lay awake and listen to the sounds of the crisis center, or I would drift off to dreamland where everything was fine. I still wanted to hurt myself, but I felt less anxious about it. I knew there was nothing I could do to hurt myself so I kind of gave up the plan and just embraced the warm, heavy blankets.

At around 6:00 the next day, a woman came into the room carrying my file.

"Okay, we are going to move you in about an hour." she said as she cleared off the trash from the table and left.

I began to panic. I had to go home. I had to leave. The windows were covered in hard plastic. There was nothing to break them. The door was metal. Every door was locked. I had to leave. I stood up and walked to the doorway of the room.

"I don't want to go." I said to the man behind the desk as I started to cry.

"It's going to be okay, it's not bad back there." he assured me.

"I know. But I don't want to go. I want to go home. I want to go home." I cried.

"Yes, but when we sent you home you came back so it's obvious that you need to be here." he said as he rolled back in his chair and crossed his legs.

"I want to go home. I want to go home. I WANT TO GO HOME!" I repeated over and over in between sobs.

"Do you want something to help you calm down?" he asked. "I can get an order from the doctor."

I nodded my head and headed back to the bed where I sat down and cried. I wanted to go home so badly. I knew how it was back there. It was torture. This room was torture. I wanted to go home and curl back up in bed under my own blankets. Some time later, a woman approached my bed and held out a small blue pill. She named off what it was and explained that it would help me relax. I took the pill and swallowed the cup of water she had brought. Before I knew it, my bones felt like rubber. My mind slowed down. I laid on the bed. I knew that I had to go into the back. I accepted it and closed my eyes.

"Okay, let's go." a man said as he entered the room. I opened my eyes and stood up. I followed him through a locked door and into a large room. I recognized my surroundings. It was always the same. I knew the process.

Just like I expected, we reviewed my inventory, put my phone in the safe, washed all the clothes I brought and they gave me my book. Then, that was it. I was free to go join the rest of the patients. I got up and looked around me. It was the same type of people as last time. Some seemed completely zoned out and drooling. Others colored pictures or sat on benches in the small grassy area outside. I wanted to go lay in the bed but I knew that the bedroom doors were locked and wouldn't open until later on in the afternoon. I decided to find a chair at the table and I began to read my book. But I couldn't read. I repeated the same paragraph over and over again. I couldn't focus. I was so tired.

I laid my head down on the table and closed my eyes. I fell asleep slowly as the white noise around me lulled me to dream land. I woke up to some loud voices around me and I sat up.

A man was arguing with a nurse. He was supposed to have seen the doctor by now but it was explained that the doctor was behind and it would be any time now. The man grumbled as he stormed off and sat down on the sofa in front of the tv. My book sat on the table, untouched. I decided to color. The only activity that I could do absentmindedly while zoning out. I decided to color a flower. There was only a small collection of broken crayons. I knew that they didn't allow pencils. I began to color the picture and I zoned out. I thought about my life. I thought about my plan for last night. I knew that it would have ruined my family. When I thought about it, I saw my daughter's face. The painful face she would make when she would find out I had committed suicide. I zoned out and colored. Several hours passed and it was dinner time. I joined the group in the dining area. Tonight's dinner was mystery meat, a bowl of rice, a dinner roll, iceberg lettuce and a carton of milk. On the side was vanilla pudding in a styrofoam bowl. I ate as much as I could force down and I threw the rest away. I knew the rooms were open so I headed to room 3, where they had assigned me. I walked in and there were three beds, one in front of me and two down the sides. There wasn't room for anything else. Except a small nightstand at the head of each bed. I put my book away and laid on the empty bed to the right. The mattress was a plastic mat that reminded me of the mats toddlers sleep on in day care. The blankets were an oversized thick white sheet and a soft cotton blanket. I curled up and closed my eyes.

A woman entered the room and I opened my eyes. She didn't say anything but she headed to a bed and she put some papers in the nightstand that I assumed was hers. She straightened out the blankets on her bed and took off her shoes. She seemed to be doing the same thing I was doing as I saw her lay in bed even though the sun was still up. I closed my eyes again.

I woke up some time later when someone was announcing that there was dessert on the counter. My stomach grumbled so I decided to see what they had. It was a pack of graham crackers. I decided to pass. I went back to the room where I laid back down but this time I pulled the blankets over myself. My roommate snored and now a second woman had entered the room and was laying on her bed. I fell asleep and woke up to a dark room. It was silent. The lights were all turned off and only the sounds of paperwork and typing came from the front desk. I wished I was at home. I missed feeling my husbands skin against mine. I looked at my watch. It was 1 in the morning. I laid on my left side and waited for him to curl up with me any second, but he never came. Instead I laid there under the blankets and cried. I wanted to go home.

The next day, I was reminded about the dreaded god forsaken vitals. At 5:00 a.m., all the patients were woken up and we stood in a single file line at the front desk. One by one our vitals were taken and we were released into the main room. The news played on the tv so I sat down and watched for a while. There was a football game at the college and the weather was going to be hotter than yesterday.

"Coffee!" someone said from the kitchen.

"Coffee?" Iasked. "Coffee!" I beelined for the kitchen where I poured myself a styrofoam cup of decaf coffee with lots of sugar. I took a sip and smiled for the first time in days. I sat back down on the couch and watched the news until the talk shows started. Breakfast was served (a boiled egg, canned pears, a small styrofoam bowl of bran flakes and a carton of milk). I ate everything.

As I threw my mess in the trash bin, someone announced "Showers!" from the kitchen and put sets of towels and one-time-use soap and toothpaste. I decided to take a shower to kill time. After I got dressed and headed to the main room with my book, I heard them go around and lock all the bedroom doors. I sat down on the couch and zoned out. I wanted to lay down but an elderly man was sitting next to me snoring while sitting up. I started to write a story in my head and after rewriting it several times, I decided to get it down on paper. I knew that the hospital legally had to provide me with a writing utensil and paper, so I went to the counter where I asked for paper.

I sat down at the table and began to write the story. I was deep in my story when I heard someone pull a chair out from directly in front of me. A woman sat down and I made eye contact and looked back at my paper.

"Hello. I'm Rebecca." she said as she pointed to her ID badge. "I'm a social worker and I wanted to get to know you. How are you doing this morning?"

"Okay." I lied as I put the crayon down.

"Okay okay, or "okay"?" she asked.

I cracked a smile

"Okay, so not okay I guess. I'm not okay." I said.

"Good. I'm glad that you recognize that." she said. "So what brings you here?"

I explained the previous 48 hours. She nodded and asked me questions. We talked for about an hour. At the end of our conversation, she said that she really enjoyed talking to me and she was glad that there was someone at the hospital that she could talk to. She got up and left and I returned to the story I was working on before.

Hours later, it was dinner time and I was starving. This time it was a huge scoop of mixed vegetables, thinly sauced spaghetti noodles, a piece of bread and a bowl of rice. They had juice this time. After dinner, I went and laid in my bed. I closed my eyes and thought about all the reasons why I didn't want to exist.

"Hey" I heard a voice say. I opened my eyes.

"I'm Roberta. Who are you?" she asked.

"I'm Sarah" I said as I sat up. I recognized her from the night before. She had slept in the bed parallel to mine.

"Do you have any kids?" she asked as she sat on her bed. She held a thick bible with a bookmark.

"Yeah. I have three." I said.

"I have a son. He is 11. He doesn't live with me though. He lives with my mom. I'm trying to get him back though." she said and looked down.

"My daughters don't really live with me. They come on the weekends now." I said. "Is that your son?" I asked when I saw the picture of the boy taped to the wall above her bed. She had photos taped up as well as coloring pages she had colored. It reminded me of a child's bedroom wall.

"How long have you been here?" I asked.

"Two months." she said. "I put my arm through a glass window because I was delusional and thought my husband was cheating on me. The cops came and now they won't let me go home because I've been here too many times. I have a hearing on Monday though. I might get to go home if I can find a board and care home that will accept me."

"Oh" I said. "I hope they let you go home."

"When do you get to go home?" she asked as she opened up her bible.

"I don't know. Maybe a couple days." I said. I knew that telling Rebecca in the morning that I still felt like hurting myself would add more time to my stay.

"Oh. Okay. I'm going to read now." She said as her eyes drifted to page.

"Okay, have fun." I said as I got up and headed to the main room. The tv was set to an evening gameshow and their was one seat open on one of the sofas so I sat down and watched. No one seemed to have control of the remote. The tv itself was locked in a clear bullet proof case. Everything was locked down. I watched tv until it was time to go to bed. When I woke up the next day for the dreaded vitals, I felt okay. I looked forward to the coffee. I wondered what monstrosity they were going to have for breakfast. I got a cup of coffee and immediately sat down at the activity table to color a picture. I sipped my coffee and colored a few pages before turning them over and writing a poem on the back. After scarfing down breakfast, I returned to the table to finish my writing.

"Hey you." I heard a voice say. I looked up. It was Rebecca, from the day before.

"How are you this morning?" she asked.

"Okay." I said. I smiled. "Okay Okay."

"Good! Glad to hear. What happened?" she asked as she sat down in the chair across from mine.

"I don't know. I just woke up this morning feeling not as depressed. I looked forward to the coffee. I don't feel like crying right now, so that's good." I said. I wasn't lying.

We began to talk about the stress of being a mother and wife. She explained that last night, her son had gotten arrested. She shared that she had been up all night with her son.

"See, we all have stuff going on. You're not alone by any means." she said. "I take antidepressants. I started taking them five years ago. It's okay." she smiled.

I shared with her my suicide plan. I shared my reasoning for coming back and I shared with her why I had lied before. I told her that I lied to the crisis center a lot because of the dozens of times that I have been in that cold white 24 hour room, I have only ever made it through the 24 hours three times. Every other time I lied and said I wanted to come home. I was too scared. We talked for a couple of hours. She left to go work on her paperwork and I returned to my writing. Soon, my name was called from the front desk and they told me to have a seat. I sat down opposite of a man wearing a lab coat.

"Hello, I am Dr. Small the on-call doctor for the hospital today. I see that your doctor is Dr. Schnoor and he has you on some medication." he said as he rattled off the names and I nodded to confirm that I was taking them.

"So how are you doing today?" he asked. I knew that my response to this questions determined when I would go home.

"I'm doing better. I don't feel as depressed today. I still feel like hurting myself though." I said and looked down.

"Ah, I see." he said as he typed a few things on the computer in front of him. "Okay, well, I have reviewed your medication and it seems that you're on a good regimen. There's really not any changes I can make."

"Oh I wasn't looking to make changes." I said. "I was just suicidal."

"Okay. Well, how about we check back in tomorrow and see how you're doing?" he said and smiled at me.

Our appointment ended and I headed back to the activity table where I had left my writing. Soon it was lunch, then dinner, then bed time. A few new people joined the group and some old people were released. The third girl in our room had been replaced by a woman with red hair but I hadn't gotten the chance to see her face yet because she arrived in the middle of the night.

Once the vitals were done in the morning, I headed back to the bedroom to get my book and see if I could focus enough to read it. Probably not but I could try at least. I decided to read in the room until they called for breakfast.

"My hearing is today." Roberta said. I looked up from my book. She was wearing a button down blouse and a broomstick skirt. "I'm nervous."

"Good luck!" I said. "I hope it goes well for you."

"They're supposed to come get me when it's time but I don't know when that is." she said as her eyes darted around the room.

"Maybe you could ask them" I suggested.

"Yeah, I'm going to go ask." she nodded and headed out the door. I returned to my book.

"Hey, I'm Miranda." a woman said as she walked in the room and sat on the third bed.

"Hi" I said.

"Did you do it?" she asked.

"Do what?" I asked.

"Commit suicide." she said. "Well, try to at least."

"No." I said as I looked at my feet. Of all the years that I have been suicidal, I have never attempted it in my life because ultimately, I'm afraid of death and pain.

"I did. In my garage. My fucking daughter thought she would go out and do what she wants so I had to show her that the world doesn't revolve around her." Miranda said as she showed me the rope marks on her neck.

"Oh." I said, shocked.

"Yeah, I should be released tomorrow though so oh well." she said and shrugged.

I went back to my book and she left the room. Breakfast came around and I didn't even care what the food was anymore, I was just hungry. I ate everything.

The main door was unlocked and Roberta came in sobbing. They locked the door behind her and she headed towards the room. I followed her.

"What happened?" I asked.

"There is no hearing. They've already put a hold on me. I'm staying her for at least 45 more days." she said as she sobbed and wiped her wet face.

"Oh, I'm so sorry." I said. She sobbed. I didn't know what to do.

"Do you want to play a game with me?" I asked.

"No" she said as she pulled her covers back. "I'm just going to go to sleep. They will have to drag me out of here when they lock the doors."

Lunch and dinner passed quickly and soon the evening news was on and I was coloring at the table again. Rebecca came and sat down.

"How are you doing?" she asked.

"Good!" I said and smiled. I felt okay. I didn't feel like I was going to fall apart anymore.

'Awesome. Did you see the doctor today?" she asked.

"Yes." I responded. "I told him I was feeling a little better. Not all the way though."

Rebecca talked to me about my family. She brought up her own struggle with depression and what she uses to keep herself grounded. We laughed at ourselves and soon she had to return to work but she told me that she would rather talk to me than go back to paper work. I smiled. Bed time came and I slept. I missed the warmth of my husband's body. My pillow was consistently wet all night long as I cried myself to sleep and then woke up in the middle of the night to cry some more.

The following day was just like the previous. I saw the doctor and I reported that I was actually feeling much better. He was pleased and mentioned that I may be going home the following day if things continued to look promising. I was hopeful. The day slowly passed. I couldn't focus on the tv or the book so I colored at the table and wrote poetry on the back of the pages. By the end of my stay, I had a stack of coloring pages that I had done.

The next day, the front desk called for me to see the doctor. I reported that I was feeling much better and I was ready to go home. He agreed that I seemed to be doing fine and he would begin the process of discharging me. He said to expect to leave in a few hours. I was completely delighted. I couldn't stop smiling. I couldn't wait to go home. I called my husband from the patient phone and told him the good news. A few hours later, I was escorted to the entrance of the hospital where my husband greeted me. He was wearing a shirt with cut off sleeves and a pair of old shorts.

"I see that you got dressed up." I said, teasing him.

"Yard work" he said and winked.

We got in the car and I immediately lit up a cigarette. I began to smoke and feel the breeze hit my face as the car moved down the street.

"There's something I need to tell you." he said as he drove towards our house across town.

"Yeah?" I said.

"Yeah." he said. He cleared his throat. "Some stuff was said about you. While you were gone." He told me who it was, and who had heard it. He continued.

"They said that you didn't deserve to get fast food. You shouldn't have been rewarded with a friend coming to visit you. You "put yourself there."

They have "zero sympathy". They said you did it for attention. It was in front of a group of people." He named off who was there.m. Not many stood up for me. Actually, no one really did. The subject was just changed and I was ignored.

"I'm sorry." he said. "I just thought that you should know."

I was silent. He didn't know but my heart had just broken into a thousand pieces. Someone that was supposed to love me unconditionally was treating me like I had put myself in jail. They acted like I had robbed a bank and been arrested. I was so angry but I didn't say anything. I just stewed with the thoughts in my head.

When we got home, I felt weak. I recognized the feeling of being weak and fragile after being in the hospital. Everything was so loud and bright. I went to my room as soon as we got home. Later, my husband came in to check on me.

I was sobbing hysterically at the foot of our bed.

"Why?!" I shouted. "Why would they say that about me? I didn't do it for attention. I didn't want to go. I didn't want to be there. You know that! I cried every fucking day. It's miserable there. I cried myself to sleep because all I wanted was to be at home with you. I didn't do it for attention. I had to go." I sobbed into my hands.

He tried to console me but it was no use. I was hysterical. I cried off and on for days. My heart was broken. My relationship with this person was ruined. It would never be the same. I had lost a person within my inner circle on that day. The list of the people that truly supported me became shorter.

A year after my release from the hospital, I saw the social media posts in the past events section. It triggered my memories from when my heart was ripped out of my chest after I had gotten out of the hospital. I cried for hours even though a year had passed. I will always mourn that broken relationship with that person.

When the one year mark came and went, I celebrated I had been taking me meds consistently for a year which means I had not had any major bipolar depressive episodes in a year. Of course my symptom list is a mile long so there were many other things to worry about, but at least I hadn't been suicidal to the point of needing to be hospitalized.

Disability

I think I scoffed at the term "disability" when it was first used to describe mental illnesses. However, as time has gone on, I have seen the reasons why mental illnesses are disabilities and it is because these conditions are disabling. I never thought I was disabled. I thought I was doing just fine! But, as I found out in 2015, I was not "fine". I was miles from "fine".

When I had my manic and depressive episode in 2015 that caused me to lose my job, I initially wanted to stay at home to take a break. I was skating on thin ice and I had only gotten my job because I had a good reference. All of my bridges were burned and I am certain if past employers were asked if they would hire me again, they would immediately say "no".

I began working at COV when I was 19. I was newly engaged and full of life. At first, I seemed like a great employee and I was a great addition to the team. But over time, it became apparent that I had some issues going on that often got in the way of work.

I would grow paranoid sometimes and believe that other coworkers were out to get me. I believed that they were all plotting against me to get me fired. If I walked into a room and they were laughing, I believed they were laughing at me. My mind would often pick a target and I would slowly grow to hate them which created a conflict between us when there was never anything wrong in the first place.

I often had breakdowns at work. There were times that I would begin sobbing in the middle of working or cry in the parking lot before I went in. I called in sick anytime I felt depressed, which was often. I had panic attacks when assigned with challenging clients and I have had breakdowns in the bosses office and they asked me to leave the building. I have become manic and started projects at work that were never finished and I would become obsessed with a certain task at work to then abandon it the next day. I had such a habit of not finishing projects that I was asked to please not present any more ideas unless I have completed them first.

During the 8 years that I worked there, my position moved from part-time to full-time to assistant manager and back to part-time. I eventually ended up in a part-time position again and I was determined to be full-time. So I applied for every position available. I interviewed for it six times over the course of two years. The last time I interviewed for the position, I was the only person applying for the position, but they decided to close the opening instead. I was devastated. But I also remember I was manic during the interview and wore a much-too-small mini dress to the interview because I was convinced that the director wanted to have an affair with me. Later, a friend of mine browsed my employee file one day and found that they was a note. It said that I was "mentally unstable". I was incredibly offended. They were obviously wrong! I was fine!

I was working at PC, another company, when I had my manic episode in 2015. I struggled to make it to work, complete paperwork and maintain consistency. I loved my job but I cried on my way to work every day because it was so challenging to me. When I stopped working, I didn't apply for unemployment because I didn't think I would get it. I was encouraged to apply for state disability which was very simple to get. It only lasted for a year and the paperwork advised that you apply for long term Social Security Disability Income if you see your disability being long term.

I wasn't going to apply because I felt like it would be ripping everyone off. I didn't see myself as disabled and I didn't think I deserved it. But a friend told me to apply anyway "because you never know where you'll be in two years". So I applied and forgot about it. Six months later I got a letter of denial. I wasn't shocked, I was expecting it. Knowing the process pretty well, I immediately contacted a lawyer and handed my case over to them. They took care of everything for me and only contacted me for signatures or to update me on the process. After the third denial, the law firm requested a hearing for me. I was given a date of August 24th. The day before my son's birthday.

The day of the trial, I was shaking. I had written out my day-to-day activities like they had asked. I described my daily panic attacks and how debilitating my depression was. I told them all of my medications and they read all of my medical records. I was so nervous about the trial that I vomited in the car.

Once in the courthouse, I was met by my lawyer. She reviewed the case documents and we talked. I told her about my decision with my daughters and she wrote it down on a piece of paper. I also told her about other things that had happened recently which may be used as more evidence.

Once we were in the courtroom, I was taken to a chair at a table with a microphone. I was instructed to speak clearly into the microphone. I swore that I would tell the whole truth, nothing but the truth, so help me god. There was a transcriber at a computer, an employment expert on speaker phone, a judge sitting at the front of the room and my lawyer and I sitting opposite. At first, the judge and lawyer talked. I sat there. They discussed things in code and I wasn't quite sure what they were talking about. I found out that my recent hospital stay (1 month ago) had not be input into my medical documents so they had to request the information. I sat there at the table and just listened along.

Then, the judge addressed me. She asked me to go through my routine and asked me questions. I explained that some of my days are debilitating and I am unable to get out of bed while other days I have a good day and I am able to function. She told me to focus on the days when I can't function. I explained my frequent (daily) panic attacks. I described being too depressed to go to work. I laid everything out on the table.

Then, the lawyer began to address me. She asked me to explain my decision with my daughters. I began to explain the situation and my eyes filled with tears. My lawyer asked about my parents living next door and why I have to send my son over there so often. My lawyer asked why I had not driven to the trial and she asked me to go into detail about my suicidal thoughts. By the end of the hearing, I felt naked and exposed. My eyes were damp from crying and I felt so ashamed. Everyone in the room knew my medical history and my dark secrets. I felt like the size of a mouse. But then, the hearing was over. My lawyer and I were excused and as we headed out the door the judge said "You're almost there!" which hinted that she ruled in my favor.

Two months later I checked the mail and found a large envelope from the Social Security office. My husband asked me to open it inside but I was too excited. I opened it in the driveway and saw the words "FULLY FAVORABLE" and I knew that I had won. I felt like I was in shock. It was such a relief to finally be done with this process as I was ready to move on.

However, my mind began to take off. Over the course of 24 hours, I became incredibly depressed. I sobbed into my pillow at the thought of being "disabled". I sobbed for my wasted education and my career that I had lost. I was devastated to be considered disabled and unable to work. $17,000 was deposited into my bank account one day. It was all of my backpay in one lump sum. I sobbed. I didn't want the money. I didn't want any of it. I wanted to be better. I wanted to work at a job like a real adult. I didn't want to spend my life sitting at home. I cried for days.

Tuesday
The alarm sounds off at 5:20
"I ain't what you're used to. I don't mess with these dudes.." the phone sang. My husband hit the snooze button.
The alarm went off again at 5:27.
"I ain't what you're used to. I don't mess with these dudes.." Snooze.
5:35
"I ain't what you're used to. I don't mess with these dudes.." Snooze.
5:45
"I ain't what you're used to. I don't mess with these dudes.." Snooze.
 He finally gave up at 5:50, jumped out of bed and threw his clothes on.
"I have to go, I'm going to be late." he said as he kissed my forehead as I stretched in bed.
"Every morning!" I said as he headed out the bedroom door. I headed towards the coffee pot in the kitchen. We said goodbye and he went to work. I poured my first cup of coffee and headed out back where I smoked, drank my coffee and browsed my phone. After about an hour passed, I came inside and got dressed. I turned on my son's bedroom light and I began to sing to him.
"Good morning to you.
You smell like a shoe.
Good morning good morning.
Goooooooooood morning to you."
By the end of the song he was giggling and rolling around in bed. He got out of bed and I made him breakfast. He sat in front of the tv and watched cartoons while I began to clean up the front of the house.
It had already started when I had woke up. The nausea came almost as soon as I opened my eyes. It hit like a ton of bricks and it weighed me down. Slowly as the morning went on, it grew worse and worse. Some days it was worse than others. Today was a bad day.

As I walked around the living room picking up toys, I started to be consumed with thoughts of vomiting. I sat down on the couch and breathed slowly and deeply. I had 20 minutes before we had to be out the door so I begged myself to get it together. Thankfully my son was being independent that morning and he had gone and gotten dressed on his own. I closed my eyes and sat on the couch. The whole world was spinning and I was beyond the point of needing to throw up.

"Mommy can't drive today. We have to walk" I told my son as I got off the couch and headed towards the entry way.

"But I want to drive!" He demanded. I knew why. It was cold and damp. But I could barely walk.

"Sorry buddy, we have to walk." I said and handed him his backpack. We headed out the door and turned left on the sidewalk which we followed all the way to school. I was so relieved when I dropped him off at the entrance because I knew that he would go have fun and grow but mostly, I knew that he would stay away from me, a monster. He needed to be away from me.

After I returned home, my husband video called me. I told him about my nausea. I told him that I could barely walk to the school and I had tried to eat but I couldn't force myself to swallow. He gave me a few ideas to try but I had already tried them.

"How's work?" I asked, changing the subject.

"Okay." he said. He explained a catastrophe at work that he was having to deal with as well as the uncooperative customers that made his job harder. Soon he had to return to work and we hung up.

I sat on the couch with violent vomiting images running through my mind on a loop. I breathed slowly and deeply and I closed my eyes. I knew that I had to clean but the nausea was too intense. My anxiety filled my head with thoughts of vomiting and sickness. I paced the hallway with my hands on my head. I began to cry and I breathed through my mouth. I felt awful, but I knew that I had to go lay down. I felt like the laziest person to ever exist. I was furious with myself.

I usually have to take a nap halfway through the day. Being awake is so exhausting and I have to break up the day into parts is too overwhelming. I have to take a nap almost every day and I hate it. I am so ashamed.

I closed the curtains and shut the door. I laid down and soon fell asleep. I slept for an hour. Once I woke up, the nausea was gone and I felt better. I began to clean the house but I was finished soon afterwards. I lost my motivation to do anything beyond zone out on the couch. I was hungry but too unmotivated to cook so I just ate a chunk of cheese and a spoonful of peanut butter. I felt like crying. The emptiness was crushing me.

I felt like my life was meaningless. There was no purpose. I was so angry at myself for sleeping my life away. I was wasting my life cleaning the house and pacing the hallway with anxiety. The emptiness in my chest grew so painful that I had two options; slice my thigh with a razor blade or smoke a bowl of cannabis. So I smoked. The emptiness got better and I was able to continue with my day. I tended to our animals, checked the mail and I was able to force some more food down and keep it down. My husband called again.

"Hello my beautiful gorgeous amazing wife." he said into the camera.

"Hello baby." I responded.

"How are you doing?" he asked.

"Okay. I was having a tough time earlier but I smoked and now I feel better. I haven't done anything calming yet so I think I'm going to either write or color." I said.

"Good. Are you going to be able to go pay rent today?" he asked.

"Yeah. I forgot. I guess I could go do that now. God I don't want to go. Can you go? I really don't want to go." I said as I started to panic.

"Baby I can't go, you have to take care of this." he said.

"Ugh fine. I'll call you when I get back." I said and we hung up the phone. I paced the living room for a few minutes before gathering the courage to go get in the car. My hands were shaking as I pulled the car out of the driveway and headed down the street. I made it to the rental place in 15 minutes but I had grown so nauseous on the drive there that I was dry heaving in the front seat. After a few minutes, I wiped my face with a napkin and got out of the car. I adjusted my clothes and went inside the building.

I was able to hold it together to talk to the receptionist. Once the business was taken care of, I came back to the car and I collapsed in the seat. I drove home and felt so relieved when I pulled into the driveway. I immediately called my husband.

"I did it!" I said into the camera. "I talked to the lady and everything."
"Good job!" he said. "I have to get back to work though. I love you."
"I love you too!" I said as I hung up the phone.
The emptiness started to creep in again. The boredom became excruciating. I smoked another bowl and began to garden in the flower beds. Soon it was time to get my son from school so I cleaned up and waited for the bell to ring before I walked to the pathway two houses down.
He gave me a big hug as soon as he saw me.
"Can we go to the park?" he asked.
"Maybe." I said. "Let's talk to daddy about that."
We headed home and he tossed his backpack on the couch as soon as we walked in the door. I knew that he wanted a snack and juice. He threw off his socks and shoes and turned on the computer to play Minecraft.
"Homework in twenty minutes." I said as I prepared his snack.
I did a few chores while he played his game and then we started to work on his homework. Soon my husband was home from work. I felt so relieved. My anxiety decreased significantly. I wanted to jump in his arms. I wanted to smother him. Instead I kissed his lips and hugged him. The evening carried on as usual. Our son played in the floor while we both cooked dinner. After dinner we went for a walk to the local neighborhood park. At 8:30 I read my son a story and he went to bed. My husband and I sat outside on the swing for an hour as we smoked and talked.
I'm always nervous at night time. The day has passed and I made it through, but what about the next day? Will I have a major panic attack? Will I be manic? Will I be depressed? Will I have a breakdown? Every day brings hurdles and challenges and all I can do is try my best to get through them, each and every day.

Aleesha
It was 2015. We initially talked on the phone for two hours. I explained to her that I had just experienced a manic episode and I believed I had bipolar disorder. I told her my symptoms and I told her my experience with the rotten doctor that had discarded me after telling me I had a "personality problem". She was shocked at how I was treated. She

asked me to write down all of my symptoms and we scheduled an appointment in her next available time slot.

When I got to her office, I noticed that she had positive quotes posted all around. There were family photos and little trinkets on her bookshelf. Her psychology books all had worn spines where they had been opened so many times. She was my height and she had a glorious smile.

"Hello!" she said. "Come on in."

I followed her into her office where I sat down in a chair opposite of her desk. She rolled her chair up to her desk and clicked away.

"Just a minute, we have to do some boring paperwork first." she said as she looked at the computer screen.

After all the paperwork was signed and I was logged in, she scooted away from the computer and looked at me.

"Well, where do we begin?" she asked.

So I began. I told her what had happened only a few weeks before, when I had become obsessed with opening a business and I had quit my job. I told her about being suicidal on the kitchen floor and I told her about my paranoia, outbursts, delusions and recent events that led me to believe that I had something going on.

She pulled out her books and she began to read to me. She read scenarios of patients which described how they felt and acted. I didn't relate to any of them at all. Once we approached the bipolar section however, I didn't really relate to my surprise.

"But there's more. There is Bipolar II which has a milder form of mania and severe depression." She read off the scenario of the patient, a writer who struggled with hypomanic periods followed by depressive periods. I never related to something so much in my entire life.

That appointment, we discussed symptoms and disorders. It was pretty settled that I had bipolar but it wasn't added to my chart yet, just noted. Each appointment after that, she listened to me. She gave me different perspectives and offered advice. It was the first time I had ever sat down and talked to someone like that so it was kind of overwhelming at first.

After a year of appointments, she sat me down and explained that she would transfering to the children's department.

I hated her. I wanted to run her over with my car. She was abandoning me. How could she leave me! I was so angry.

"Are you okay?" she asked, after explaining her new job to me.

"I'm fine". I lied.
"Okay, some clients have a hard time with this. I just want to make sure you're okay." she said sweetly.
"I'm fine." I lied again. I wanted to light her desk on fire.
I completely shut down and hated her from that day forward.

Marella

I arrived in her office and she instructed me to sit in a chair.
"Not the one on the right. Sit in that chair." she said, pointing to a chair. It was completely against the wall, opposite of her desk which was completely against the opposing wall. She sat down at her desk. My instinct was to move the chair forward because she was so far away, but there was a sign that read DO NOT MOVE YOUR CHAIR FORWARD on her desk, so I restrained myself.
"How are you?" She said typing on the computer. She didn't look at me. I hadn't seen her in a month.
"I'm fine." I said as a reflex.
"Good" she said as she typed. "Is there anything you want to talk about today?"
"I've been really depressed lately. I've been having a hard time getting out of bed." I said and lowered my head.
"You should go for a walk. Go around your neighborhood and look at all the pretty flowers and trees." she said without looking up from her computer.
"What?" I asked.
"Go for a walk." She stopped typing and looked at me. "You need to get out of the house. It will make you feel better."
I started to cry.
"How the hell do you expect me to go for a walk when I can barely get out of bed? How about some realistic advice like maybe I should try to take a shower every day or eat like I should?" I said with frustration.
"Your depression is a baby." she said as she pretended to hold an infant in her arms. "You are nurturing your depression like a baby."
"How am I nurturing it? I get out of bed every day. It may take me a few hours, or all day, but I eventually get out of bed. I try to be productive.

Today I did a load of laundry. How is that nurturing my depression?" I asked.

"You feed into it." She returned to typing on her computer and she didn't look at me. The room was silent except her typing.

"Is there anything else that you would like to talk about?" she asked without looking at me.

"No, not really." I said.

"Okay, we have only 30 minutes today so we will cut it short." she said as she pulled out an appointment card.

I didn't like her. She was mean. She used tough love. She blamed me for my problems. I was only aware of Bipolar Disorder so I had no idea about BPD yet. But she treated me like I was not worthy of care. She gave me zero attention or sympathy. She never stopped typing on her computer and she only made eye contact if she needed to put emphasis into whatever unrealistic advice she was giving to me.

I filled out a transfer of care form to apply for a new therapist but before the paper could be processed, she left for a family emergency and never returned.

Monica

I sat in the small brown chair across from hers. I wanted to get a new therapist. I didn't like her. I'd given her 8 appointments to prove me wrong but I didn't think it was a good match.

"Is there anything you would like to talk about today?" she asked as she flipped through her paperwork.

"Just the same thing as before I guess. My panic attacks are becoming more severe and frequent. I now know that the anxiety is causing the nausea which explains a lot." I said. "I have been using CBD oil and I have noticed a huge difference in my anxiety but it's expensive and we can't afford it."

"Hmm. Well, like I said before. I think that your increased panic attacks are because you are getting better. They are getting more severe because you are finally allowing yourself to feel your emotions. You need to pick a time during the day to have a panic attack. Maybe at ten in the morning, go to a safe and quiet place, and say "I'm going to have a panic attack now." and allow yourself to have a panic attack at that scheduled time. If you start to have a panic attack at an unscheduled time, tell yourself to wait until the scheduled time."

I stared at her. She continued.

"The oil is probably a placebo effect. So every day, just pretend that you are taking it. Tell yourself "Okay, I'm going to take my oil now." and fool yourself into believing that you took it. Even use an empty medicine dropper. I bet you'll feel good if you do that." she said assuringly.

She completely lost me. The appointment was just me staring at her while she talked. I had already checked out. When she handed me the appointment card for our next appointment, I knew that I would be cancelling it.

After the appointment, I approached the desk and got a form to find a new therapist. I was told it would be 60 days until they assigned me to someone new. I cancelled the next appointment and decided that I was going to wait until I had a new therapist.

I also grabbed a calendar for The Wellness Center. They have 2-4 classes and support groups a day. I was planning on attending a class once my son returned to school from summer break. I wanted to start with the women's group first. There was also a mindfulness group and an art class that I wanted to check out. I knew that it was a center that was designed to help people with severe mental illness so I wanted to become involved. I posted the calendar on my fridge and counted down the days until I could start my first class.

Dr. Schnoor

I arrived in his office and he showed me to the chair. I felt so comfortable in his office. I had confessed so many things to him and he had also shared some personal stuff with me. I wished I could have him as a therapist.

"Good morning Sarah" he said with a heavy accent. "How are you today?"

"I'm okay I guess. I've been having a rough time lately." I said. "A lot of little depressions and my panic attacks are getting really bad now. It's all so overwhelming. Is there anything you can do?"

He took off his glasses and rubbed his forehead. He wiped his glasses with a cloth and began

"Sarah." He put his glasses back on. "You come into my office and you want me to help you and I want to help you but what you need to understand is that the medication is for Bipolar. And it is working, is it not? You haven't been in the hospital for over a year, correct? Recovery is not a destination, but a lifestyle."

I nodded.

"You have Bipolar Disorder, Borderline Personality Disorder and Generalized Anxiety Disorder. That is three major disorders. The medication will help you, and it is helping you, yes? But it cannot do everything. You need therapy. Lots and lots of therapy. You will be in therapy your whole life. You need to learn to cope. You need to accept your condition for what it is and go from there. You aren't going to be cured, I cannot cure you. You need to just try to live life as normally as possible. I'm sorry but you are severely mentally ill and you should not expect to be cured. Just learn to cope and try to live a normal life, ok? Your recovery begins now."

He wrote up my prescriptions for three months and I scheduled myself to see him again in three months.

I decided that I was going to start patching my holes. I was going to start going to the Wellness Center several times a week. It would be my home away from home. I was also going to join the local NAMI support group in an effort to better myself but also maybe make a friend or two. With my (eventual) new therapist, new approach and new beginnings, I will step foot on the road of recovery. I'm not sure where that road will take me, but I know where I have been. I know that some of my holes have been patched but there is so much more work to do. But with my psychiatrist, my husband, my kids and my support network, I think that progress will be made.

Manufactured by Amazon.ca
Bolton, ON